BREAD SCULPTURE

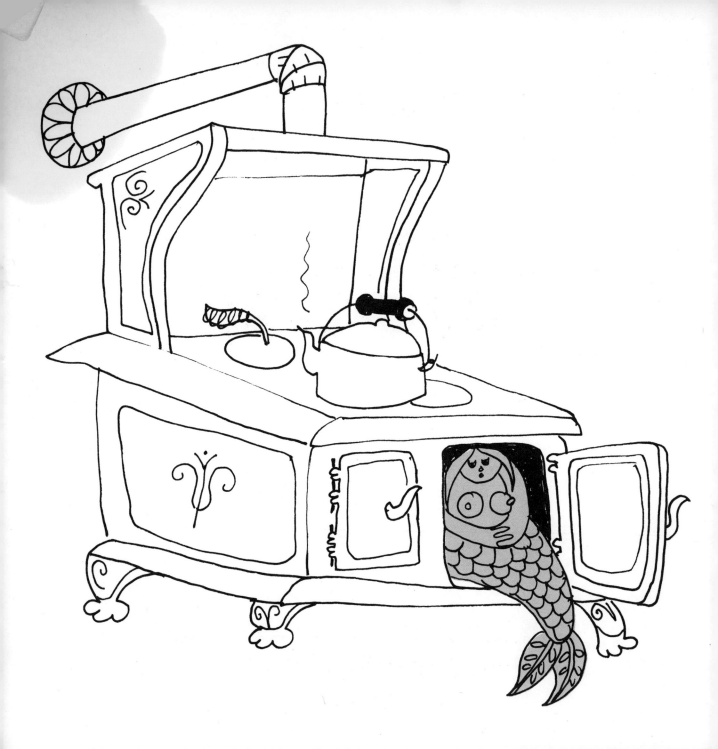

BREAD SCULPTURE
The Edible Art

Ann Wiseman

Published by 101 Productions
San Francisco
1975

to MY father

Bread Sculpture
the Edible Art
copyright 1975
Ann Wiseman ©

Illustrations
copyright ©
Ann Wiseman

Distributed to the book trade in the United States by Charles Scribners Sons new york and in Canada by van nostrand Reinhold Ltd. Toronto

Published by 101 productions 834 mission st. San Francisco california 94103

Printed in the united states of America

Library of Congress Cataloging in Publication Data

Wiseman, Ann.
    Bread sculpture.

    Includes index.
    1. Bread dough craft.   2. Bread.   I. Title.
TT880.W57   745.5   75-26909
ISBN 0-912238-74-7
ISBN 0-912238-72-0 pbk.

CONTENTS

Bread is patience

Bread is forgiveness

Bread is money

Bread is Labor

Bread is

Bread

Bread

Bread will grow, stretch & keep

Bread is caring

Bread can be any shape & yummmm

6

is love

is the staff of life

Bread is the symbol of nourishment

Bread built the pyramids of Egypt

Bread can be made from all grains & leftovers

Bread takes its form from time & fuel

Bread feeds the world

Bread makes itself

7

BARREL BREAD STORY

In the old days
Every home hoped to have
a hundred-pound barrel of flour
to last through the winter.

Bread was mixed right in the barrel:
You made a well in the flour with
your fist & dumped the liquid
in the well and stirred in the
flour until dough formed a ball.
When you could handle it without
it being too sticky, you removed
dough ball from barrel and
Kneaded it on a floured board
until smooth & springy.
Trust the Logic & you are free.....

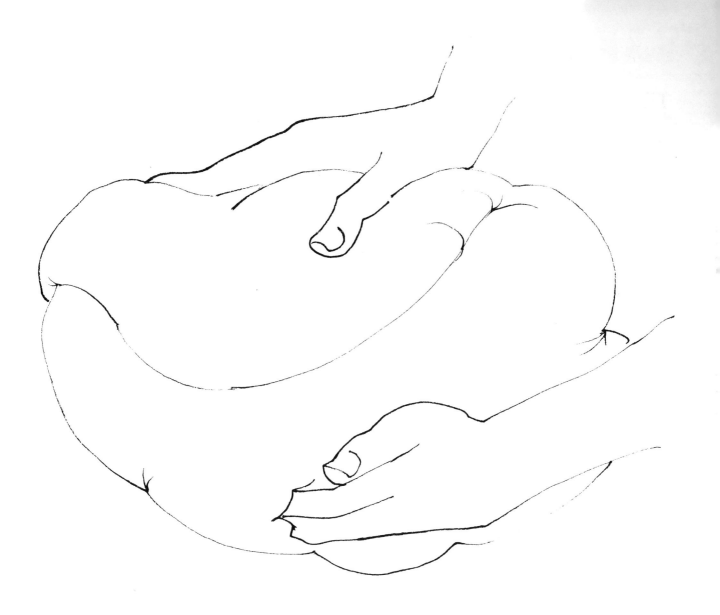

invent and create

BASIC
BREAD & SCULPTURE DOUGH

WHITE DOUGH

1 PACK YEAST
1 CUP WARM WATER
1 Tbsp. SWEETENER
1 SPILL* SALAD OIL
1 LEVEL tsp. SALT
3 CUPS UNBLEACHED FLOUR
MORE if STICKY

BROWN DOUGH

1 PACK YEAST
1 CUP WARM WATER
3 Tbsp. Molasses
1 Spill* SALAD OIL
1 tsp. SALT (to taste)
1 Cup White FLOUR
2 cups whole wheat flour

RYE DOUGH
(especially nice texture for sculpture)

1 PACK YEAST
1 CUP WARM WATER
1 Tbsp. BROWN SUGAR or HONEY
1 SPILL* OIL
3 TABLESPOONS VINEGAR
1 teaspoon SALT
1 CUP WHITE FLOUR (more for kneading)
2 CUPS LIGHT or DARK RYE FLOUR

FOR LARGER FIGURES double ingredients

* HEAPING TABLESPOON

SUPER DOUGH

2 Packs yeast
2 Cups water
2 Eggs
1/4 Cup oil
1/4 Cup honey
1 Teaspoon salt
1/2 Cup powdered milk
1/2 Cup wheat germ
1 Cup oatmeal (quick)
1 Cup granola
Add As much unbleached
   white flour to make
   dough non-sticky
   to the hands.

Knead. Raise double.
Shape or braid into
a super ring. Egg it.
Bake 1 hour or more
at 350.° W O W !

HOW-TO:

1. Pour warm water or liquid into big bowl (not too hot).

2. Sprinkle yeast & sweetener into water. Don't stir. (Hot water will <u>Kill</u> yeast & bread <u>won't</u> rise!)

3. In 5 minutes yeast will form a SCUM so you know it is alive and growing (if not-wait longer or start over)

4. Add oil or shortening & salt: About 1 scant teaspoon salt to 1 cup liquid or to taste if liquid is salted

5. Stir in ½ of the flour with a spoon. (Include wheat germ, granola, potato, purees, quick or cooked cereals, etc. at this time.)

6. When dough gets too thick to stir with spoon, turn it out onto floured board. With your hands work in as much flour as needed to be non-sticky yet springy.

7. Knead dough with confidence & authority. (Fold-Push-turn: see pp. 16 & 17) Try not to worry, wound, over-stretch or pull dough. Treat it with respect like the flesh of a good hearty friend.

8. Form dough into a ball & oil it. Set it to rise in a covered bowl in a warmish draft-free place

12

about 1 hour or until about double in size.
(Shorter if you are in a hurry — longer if you
are too busy to stop — punch it down & let it rise
again. Or if it's for tomorrow or the day after —
put it in a plastic bag in the refrigerator,
punching it down every now & then as it grows.)

9. When ready — punch dough down & knead, air
bubbles out. (If it is cold from the fridge, let it
sit & warm a bit.) Add more flour if sticky. Dough
should feel springy resilient, neither sticky nor stiff.

10. Divide dough into parts for sculpture. Cut it with
a sharp knife or scissors. Dust raw edges with flour.

11. Build sculpture lying down (unless otherwise specified)
on a greased cookie sheet or if figure is large, set
it on foil-covered oven grill (maximum size).

12. Glaze before decorating or don't glaze at all. Whole Egg
makes a golden shine. Oil = soft brown crust. Milk or water
makes a solid matte crust. EXPERIMENT....

13. Decorate & snip with scissors. Rest 5 min. (Dough will
rise as you sculpt but too much will distort shapes.)

14. Bake according to size at 350°. Cool on Rack. EAT while Fresh.

DOUGH LOGIC
GIVES YOU FREEDOM
FROM RECIPES

- LIQUID DETERMINES BULK
- YEAST OR SODA RAISES & LIGHTENS DOUGH
- SUGAR FEEDS YEAST
- SALT TO TASTE
- KNEAD TO SMOOTH
- RAISE TO DEVELOP VOLUME & TEXTURE
- BAKE ACCORDING TO COLOR & CRUST
- SCULPTURE FOR THE OCCASION
- EAT WHILE THE MAGIC IS FRESH

RULE
OF
THUMB

DOUGH IS FLOUR & WATER

APPROXIMATELY

1 PART LIQUID
TO
3 PARTS FLOUR

feel free to substitute,
improvise, adapt, enrich,
and invent your own dough!

KNEADING

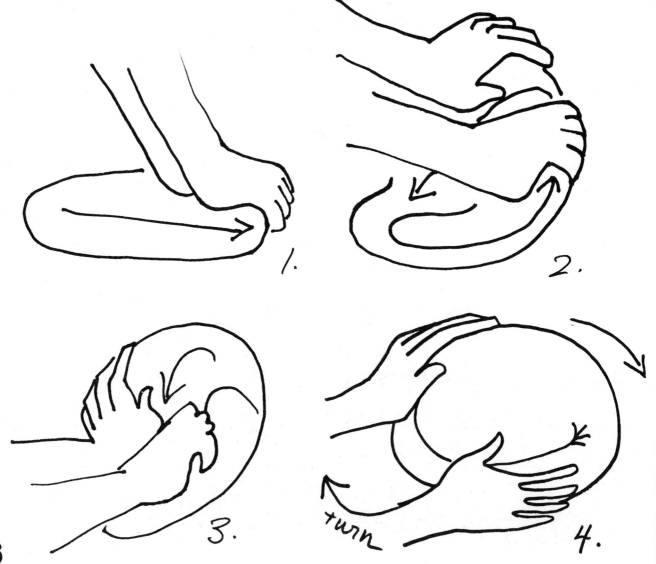

1.

2.

3.

twin 4.

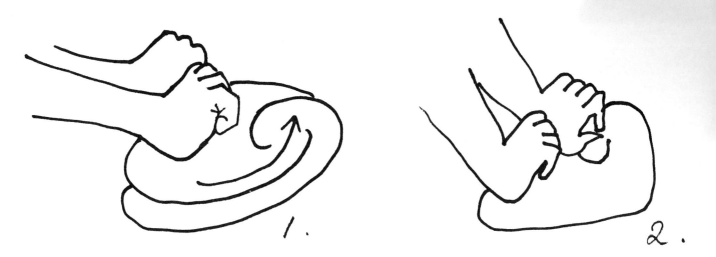

Fold dough over, pushing it into itself again and again. Fold and turn, fold and turn.

If air bubbles are big when you cut it open, knead some more.

17

INVENT YOUR OWN DOUGH

FLOUR: use some white & experiment with mixed
  flours: Rye, wheat, soya, Rice, Potato, Barley etc.
  cereals: oat meal, corn meal, cracked wheat,
      Granola, & mashed-up leftovers.
  Pureed vegetables: potato, grated fresh,
      cooked or mashed. spinach, beets, etc.
      (Lessen liquid accordingly.)

LIQUID: (always warm)
  Water   Broth   tomato juice
  Milk   beer   orange juice
  Soup   Gruel   yogurt, ETC.

YEAST: 1 pack = 1 Tablespoon dry or 1 oz. fresh.

SWEETEN (or not, yeast will rise anyway): Brown or white
      Sugar, Honey, Molasses, syrup, etc.

FLAVOR: salt yeast-water to taste. Herbs, onion, garlic, spice.

SOUR: Vinegar, yogurt, buttermilk or sour cream.

ENRICH: with powdered milk, oil, butter, Eggs, wheat
      germ, seeds, nuts, raisins, cheese, dates, fruits.

KNOW YOUR OVEN

Preheat your oven.
Bread loves even temperature.
An oven thermometer is helpful.
Allow bread to bake 15 min. before
peeking in oven, to avoid dough falling.

If crust needs extra browning
turn oven up to 400° a few minutes.
Cover areas that are brown enough
with patches of aluminum foil.

Bread when done should slide free
of greased cookie sheet or shrink
away from sides of pan.

Trust your good sense and logic
when questions arise.

Thump your knuckle on the crust
to hear if bread sounds hollow & firm.

High-rise sculpture may need more
baking time — flat ones need less.
Trust your judgement.

KNOW-HOW GUIDE

<u>CUT DOUGH</u> with sharp knife or scissors. For sculpture, the bulk of the dough is for the body. Remember to set aside enough for the parts: head, legs, arms, ears, tail & hair.

<u>DOUGH</u> is patient, it can rise & fall many times. It will wait from morning till night or a week in the refrigerator. If it goes sour it will remind you of San Francisco and Portuguese sourdough bread. <u>PUNCH</u> it down gently when it threatens to take off!

<u>IF DOUGH WON'T RISE</u> yeast may be old or killed by hot water <u>OR</u> dough may be very heavy with dark flour - give it more time. If all else fails - make a new batch of lighter dough & incorporate the two doughs. Hopefully they will rise together

<u>ROUNDING</u>: To round bodies, buns & breasts - stretch the surface gently by pushing up from underneath while smoothing the top.

<u>JOINING DOUGH PARTS</u>: Lick or wet your finger - dab both surfaces to be joined & join them. Don't make them wet, just moist & receptive.

20

SPLITTING is caused by trapped air bubbles in dough that has risen too fast or been under-kneaded. Especially on big figures try to include fork prong designs or knife cuts so steam can escape.

SCULPTURE FORMS: Simple forms & basic loaf shapes are best.

GLAZING is done with hands or brush. EGG WHITE makes crust shiny. WHOLE EGG makes it golden & shiny. WATER OR MILK makes it hard & non-shiny. KARO SYRUP makes a sweet, glossy crust; better brushed on 5 or 10 min. before end of baking time.

THE MAGIC of bread sculpture is to EAT IT FRESH or FREEZE it & reheat it later (not to hang on walls).

THE FUN is designing your own figures for your own occasions!

DECORATION & TOOLS

Decorate with nuts and seeds
especially
almonds
pumpkin seeds
sesame seeds
caraway seeds
poppy seeds
raisins
dried fruits
Dust with
paprika.
Poke with
potato peeler,
spoons, fork etc.....

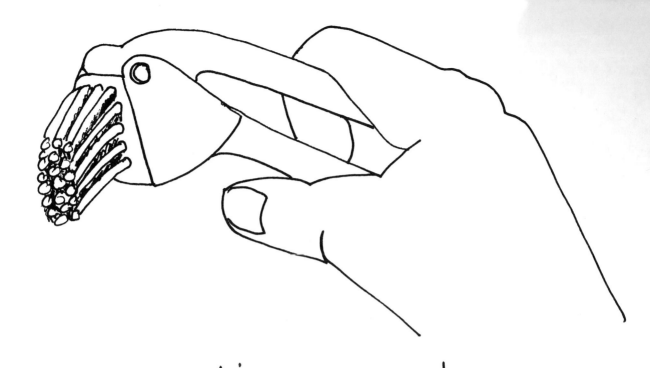

The garlic press and
the bigger-holed
lemon press make
good hair and
beards.
Squeeze dough
slowly, add more –
squeeze some more –
3 or 4 times then cut
and attach to sculpture.

23

Fork
for pronging
decorations
& air holes

Spoon
for imprinting
dove feathers,
fish scales,
& mermaid tails

scissors
for Spikes
and scales

Pastry
Brush
for Egging
glazing
oiling
or brushing
on water
to make
a "French
crust" **25**

THRIFTY BREAD

* For years and years Agnes Powers was postmistress and school teacher in Robinhood Cove, Maine.

Everyone saved stale cake, bread, pastries and donuts for her to feed her raccoons.

With New England thrift she recycled part of her stale collection into fresh bread by soaking it and steaming it and using it with Indian meal.

My son and I visited Agnes in her kitchen. We sat in silence by candlelight with the door open, waiting for her family of wild coons to come to feed while we learned about thrifty bread.

27

FLAT BREAD, UNLEAVENED

1 cup warm water
½ teaspoon salt
¼ cup oil
3 cups white or mixed flour
Mix smooth - Roll out flat ⅛"-¼"
Bake directly on oven grill or Bar B. Q grill
over grey coals or in 500° oven until toasty
on both sides.

don't worry,
if it doesn't
pocket - it is
still tasty!
try again
Hot & quick

WHEAT THINS

1 cup warm water
½ teaspoon salt
⅓ cup oil
2½ cups wheat flour
Mix smooth. Roll out flat ⅛"-¼"
Bake on hot cookie sheet or directly
on oven grill or fry in hot skillet.
28 (Toast on both sides.)

FLAT BREAD, LEAVENED

1 pack yeast
2 cups warm water
1 Tablespoon sugar
3 Tablespoons oil
1 teaspoon salt
6 cups white flour
or more - enough to be
non-sticky. Let rise
Knead. Divide into 10 balls.
Roll balls out flat on floured surface 1/8" thick.
Bake on hot cookie sheet or directly on grill
in 500° oven or on BarBQ grill over hot grey coals
until toasty on both sides.

Any basic bread dough will "pocket" when baked flat - fast & hot.

POCKET FISH

use flat bread recipe (page 29)
or basic bread dough (page 10)

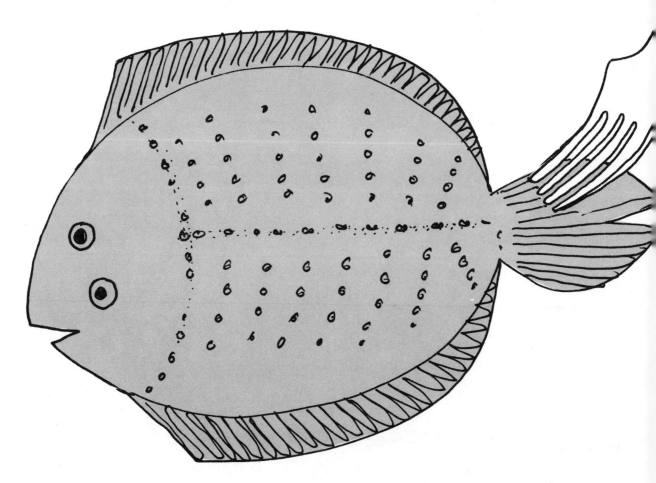

1. Divide dough into 3 or 4 tennis balls and roll out flat, 1/4" thick

2. shape fish
(dab flour on cut edges)
3. Imprint fins & tail with fork tines
4. Decorate body lightly with fork points
5. Heat cookie sheet in hot oven
6. Transfer fish to hot sheet so they bake quickly at 500° about 7 minutes

SNAKE ROLLS

This dough will keep
a week in the fridge.
(Or, use immediately.)
  1 pack yeast
  2 cups warm milk
  ½ cup sugar
  ½ cup oil
  2 eggs
  7 cups white flour
    or more
Mix & stir.
Knead until smooth.
Oil dough ball and
store in fridge, covered.
Punch down from time to time.

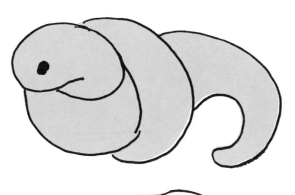

An hour before any meal,
Cut off a lump of dough.
Divide into balls.
Roll balls into snakes.
Tie snakes in knots.

Snip mouth open & add an eye.
Let snakes rise 15 minutes
on greased cookie sheet.
Bake at 400° 10-12 minutes.

OWL

Use a basic bread recipe (P.10).
After dough has risen 1 hour or so -
Divide dough into  4 parts:
① head ② body ③ wing & tail feathers
④ Legs, feet, face & ruff.
Decorate with spoon & fork.
Bake at 350° 20 to 40 min.
according to size, "thump"
& flatness of figure

35

STEGOSAURUS RYE

2 ½ cups warm water
2 packs yeast
2 Tablespoons sugar
¼ cup molasses
1 Tablespoon salt
¼ cup oil
¼ cup cocoa
3 cups rye flour
3 cups white flour

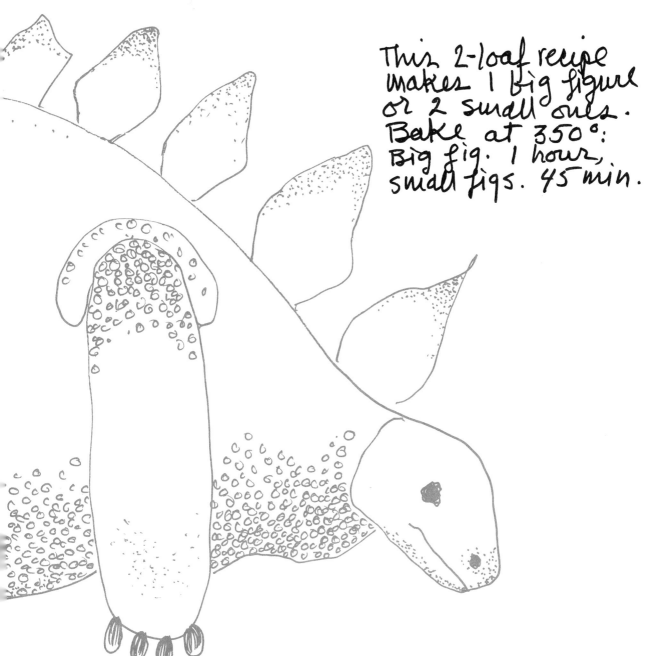

This 2-loaf recipe
makes 1 big figure
or 2 small ones.
Bake at 350°:
Big fig. 1 hour,
small figs. 45 min.

STEGOSAURUS BUILDING

1. Divide dough & shape pieces as shown.
2. Stick pieces together with wet finger.
3. Egg it & sprinkle with poppy seeds.
4. Decorate with raisins & pumpkin seeds.
   Tap paprika on spikes.

MERMAID

(GREEN SPINACH DOUGH)

1 cup warm water
1 pack yeast
1 Tablespoon sugar
¼ cup oil
1 teaspoon salt to taste
1 cup pureed spinach
3½-4 cups unbleached flour
(Rise 1 hour, add more
flour if sticky.) Knead
and Knead.

Raise
1 or 2
hours.
Shape & Bake
350° appr. 45 min.
or longer.

MERMAID BUILDING

1. Knead green dough (or use any other dough); add more flour if sticky (don't make it too dry).
2. Divide dough into 6 parts.
3. Shape body & attach parts.
4. Pat raw Egg all over mermaid.
5. Snip & raise scales with scissor points.
6. Decorate, sprinkle tail with dill or herbs.
7. Bake 35 to 50 minutes at 350°, according to thickness of figure.

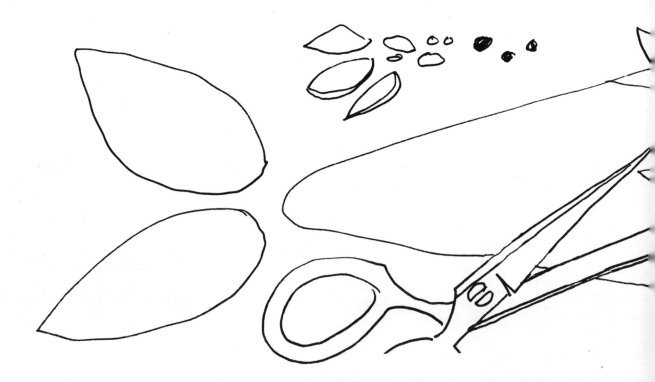

serve on a bed of parsley

LIONIZED LOAF

use any dough or try this:
2 packs yeast
2 cups warm milk
½ cup syrup (maple or honey)
1 stick melted butter
2 teaspoons salt (to taste?)
1 cup oatmeal (cooked or quick)
2 cups granola or wheat germ
5½-6 cups - unbleached flour
  until non-sticky
Knead. Let rise double.
Knead. shape. Bake at 350°
1 hour until crust is solid.

45

LION BUILDING

Make figure lying down on foil.
1. Knead dough & form sausage
2. Divide dough

leg	tail	body	head Ruff +

3. flour & shape body
   snip leg part, flour & shape
4. Add back leg & snip toes
5. Braid & attach tail
6. Flour & shape head
   Attach head & ruff

7. Egg it all over
8. Make face & decorate
9. Sprinkle seeds & paprika
10. Bake 50-60 min. according to thickness 350°

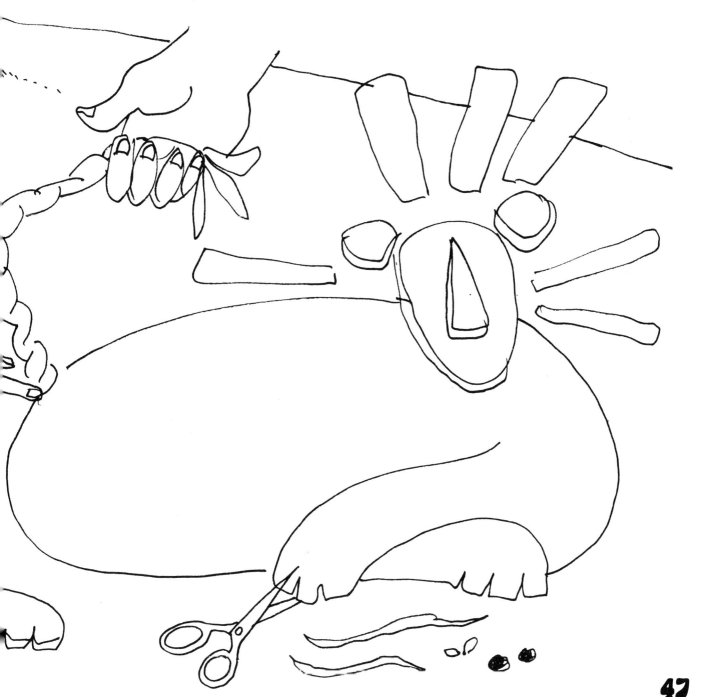

47

¼ cup warm water
2 cups warm milk
1 park yeast
½ stick butter
2 Tablespoons molasses
1 Tablespoon salt
½ cup wheat germ
1 Tablespoon caraway seeds
1 cup Rye flour
2 cups wheat flour
more white flour until
   not sticky. oil ball and
Let rise in covered bowl.

HIPPOPUMPERNICKEL

(BLACK MOLASSES DOUGH)

As this is a heavy
2-loaf recipe,
allow 2 hours slow
rising time. Knead,
Shape & Bake 375°
about 1 hour.

dark
heavy
doughs
are
some-
times
hard
to
raise

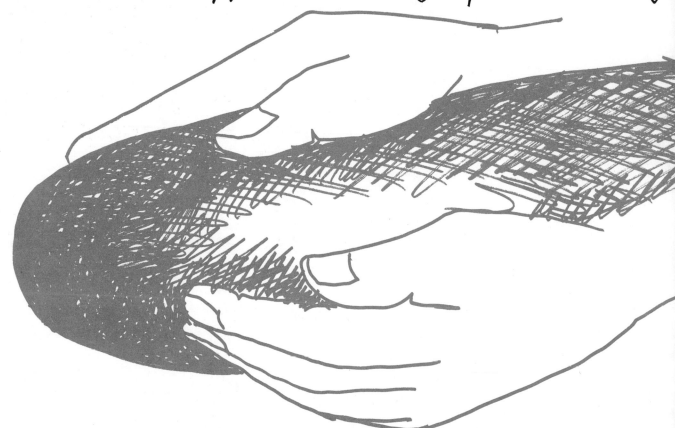

1. Knead dough smooth & cut off enough for legs (4) & ears (2).
2. Form the rest of dough into a fat sausage — heavy in the behind.
3. Form legs & ears, attach with a wetted finger. Punch nostrils.

4. Sculpture the head.
5. Glaze with egg & sprinkle seeds.
6. Allow to rise 1/2 to 1 hour.
7. Bake in 375° oven for about one hour.
8. Brush his back with water from time to time to firm crust while baking.

FERTILITY BREAD

use basic white Brown or Rye dough or pink tomato dough (p. 63)

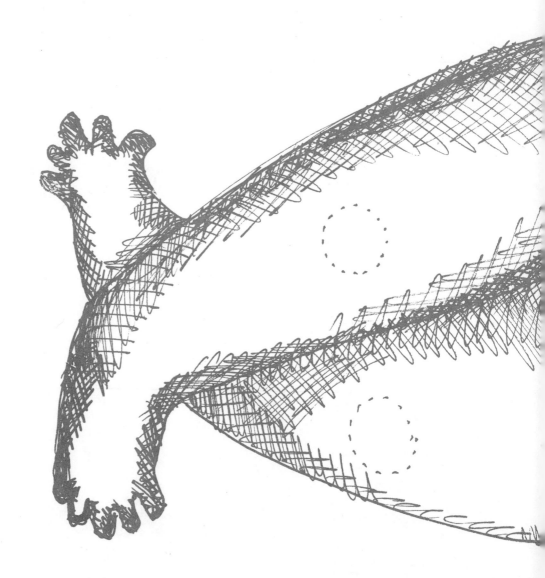

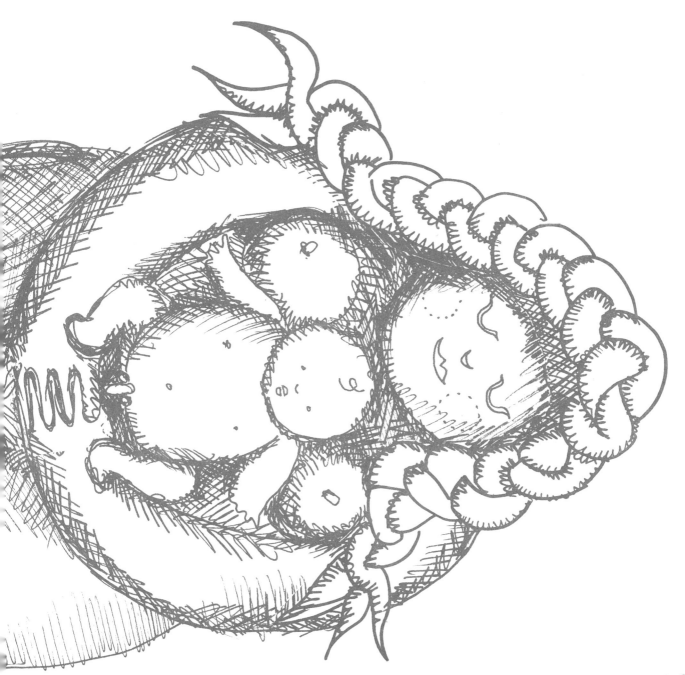

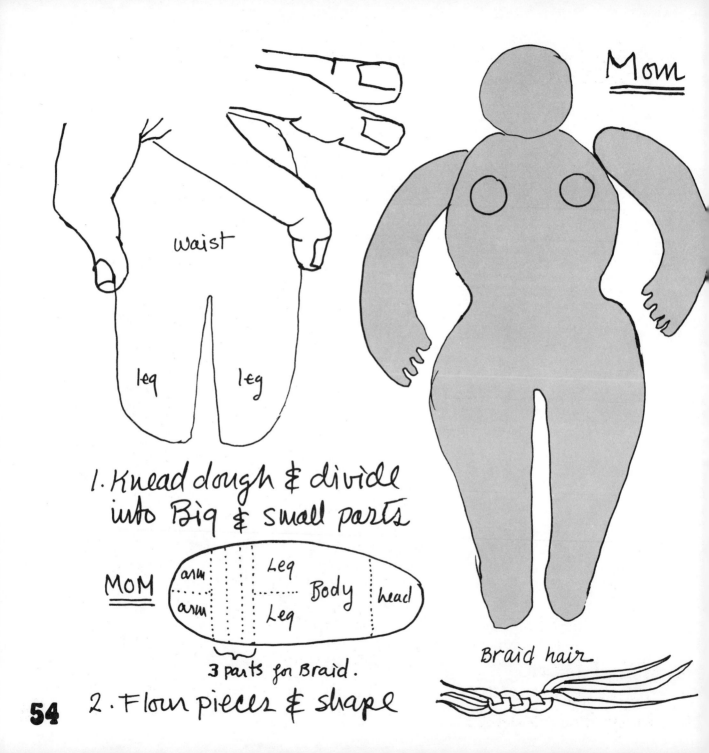

waist

leg leg

Mom

1. Knead dough & divide
into Big & small parts

MOM

arm
arm
Leg
Leg
Body
head

3 parts for Braid.

2. Flour pieces & shape

Braid hair

Baby

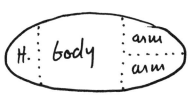

(A.)

(B.)

* Eat it fresh — while the energy is in the magic.

1. Divide sausage
2. flour & shape pieces
3. Legs can be made two ways

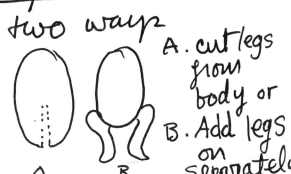

A. cut legs from body or

B. Add legs on separately

A.   B.

4. Put baby together decide if it is male or female & place in mother's arms.
5. Make a silent wish & meditate on it.
6. Egg Everything & Bake. give it to your friend. *

55

HERB & CURRY WHALE LOAF

1 pack yeast
1 cup water
1 spill* oil
1 Tbsp. soy sauce
1 Tbsp. curry powder
chopped fresh herbs
(dried salad herbs OK)
3 cups mixed flour:
    white & wheat, rye or granola
Knead · oil · rise ·
Knead · shape · oil & sprinkle with dill.
Rise ½ hour. Bake at 350° 30 - 45 min.

*Heaping tbsp.

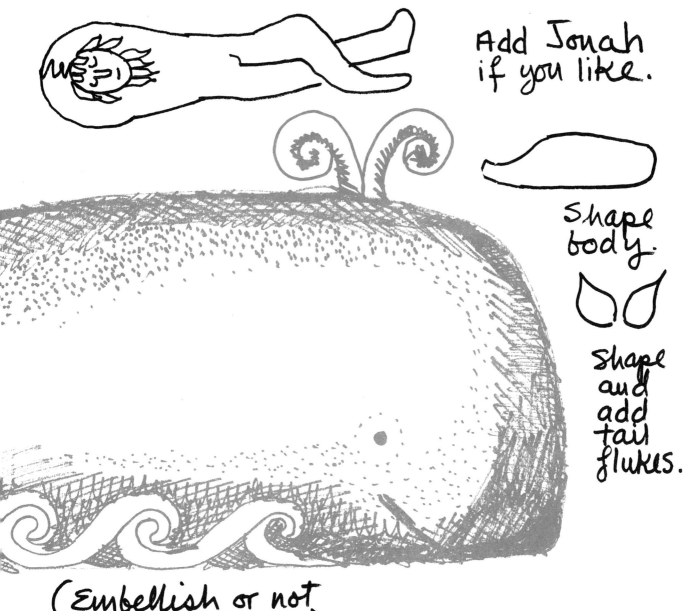

Add Jonah
if you like.

Shape
body.

Shape
and
add
tail
flukes.

(Embellish or not
as you please.)

CATCH-HER-IN-THE-RYE

Rye is a strange dough
very good for sculpture

2 packs yeast
2 cups warm water
4 Tablespoons sugar
2 Tablespoons molasses
2 spills* oil
1 spill* vinegar
1 Tablespoon salt
1 cup milk
6 - 7 cups Rye flour
Let rise 1 or 2 hours
Then work in as much
white flour as dough
needs to be un-sticky

Shape & Bake 60 min at 350° * Heaping Tbsp

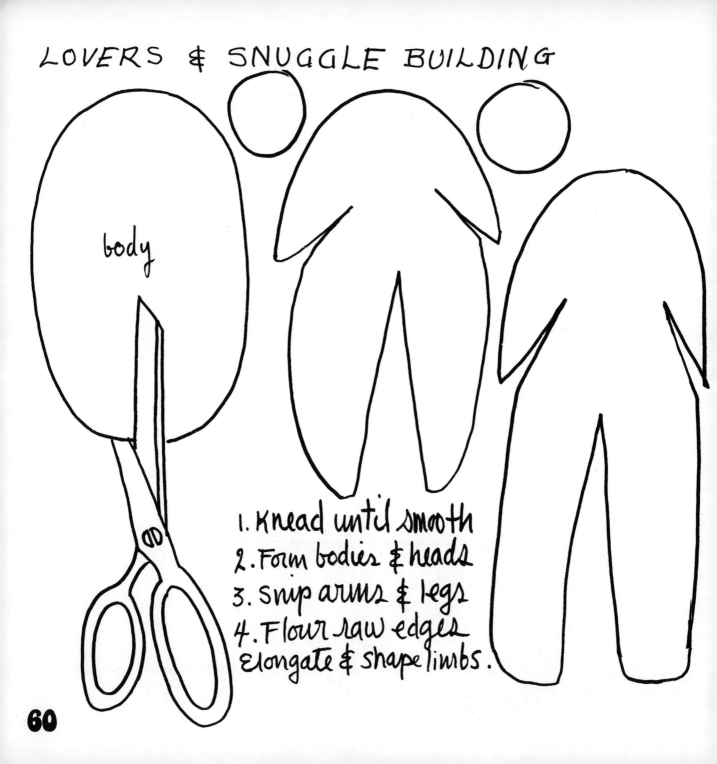

body

1. Knead until smooth
2. Form bodies & heads
3. Snip arms & legs
4. Flour raw edges
Elongate & shape limbs.

Build lovers lying down on baking sheet
5. Arrange them in any position
6. snip toes, fingers & hair
7. Egg them liberally
8. Allow them to grow together a few minutes
9. Bake them at 350° 45 to 60 minutes

PINK ANGEL
(PINK TOMATO DOUGH)

¼ cup warm water
2 Tablespoons sugar
1 pack yeast
2 cups Tomato Juice
¼ cup Catsup
¼ cup oil
1 Teaspoon salt
7½ – 8½ cups
   unbleached flour

Mix. Knead.

Rise 1 hour.
Knead. shape.
Bake 350°
45 to 60 minutes.

SWEET DRAGON RING

2 packs yeast
2 cups warm milk
½ Cup sugar
1 or 2 Eggs
2 Teaspoons salt
½ Cup oil or butter
7½-8 cups flour
        unbleached

MIX · KNEAD ·
RISE once or twice
Knead again
Shape . . . .

Make a long sausage.
Cut mouth open.
Catch tail in mouth.
Decorate & add legs.
Egg it & Bake.
350° 45 to 60 min.

BEET GRIFFIN
(RED BEET DOUGH)

1 pack yeast
½ Cup honey
1½ cups warm water
1 Cup pureed beets
1 Tablespoon salt
⅓ Cup oil
6 to 8 cups flour
unbleached. Add enough
so you can handle it
without being sticky.
Knead. Rise 1 hour.
Knead. Shape. Bake
350° about 1 hour.

Cut wings
from Red paper.

67

GRIFFIN BUILDING

1. knead Dough smooth
   cut off a part to use for legs & ears
2. Roll the rest into a long sausage
   Round the head & point the tail

3. Body can also be braided

   OR twisted

4. Make griffin standing on short legs
5. Arrange body on foil or cookie sheet

6. Shape 4 or more legs and 2 ears
7. Attach to either side of body with a dab of water
8. Punch & shape nostrils
9. Egg everything
10. Snip scales with scissors
11. Rest 20 minutes & Bake at 350° about 1 hour

Later: while still warm cut mouth open & add nut teeth

wings & fire are optional but spectacular:
cut from red paper
make slots
for wings
to slip in

CINNAMON LAMB CURLS

1 Pack yeast
2 Cups warm water or milk
1 Egg
2 tsp. brown sugar
1 Tsp. Salt
1 Stick butter
6 or more cups unbleached flour

Mix ~~together~~
Knead
Rise double
punch down
Knead again
Roll out 1/3"
Butter surface
Sprinkle sugar
+ cinnamon
cut & curl

Bake in 350° oven until toasty brown

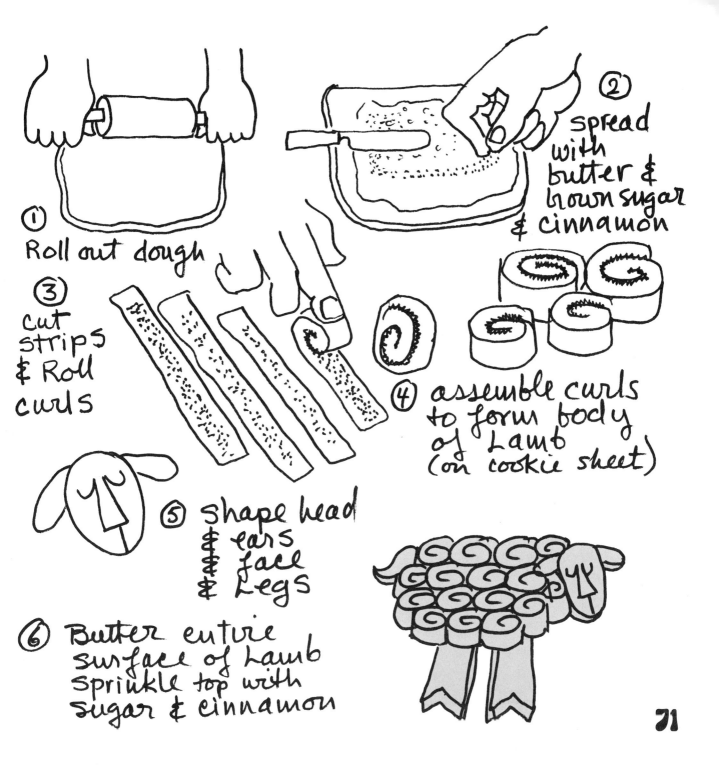

① Roll out dough

② spread with butter & brown sugar & cinnamon

③ cut strips & Roll curls

④ assemble curls to form body of Lamb (on cookie sheet)

⑤ shape head & ears & face & Legs

⑥ Butter entire surface of Lamb sprinkle top with sugar & cinnamon

HOTTENTARTS
(GARLIC & TABASCO DOUGH)

Bake 10 min. at 350°

1 pack yeast
1 cup warm water or clamato juice
1 spill* oil
1 Tbsp. Tabasco (to taste?)
1 clove crushed garlic
1 cup granola (or oatmeal or cornmeal)
2 cups white flour (more if needed)
Knead all together. Rise double.

① cut dough in 5 or 10 bodies & heads. Flatten bodies & roll head balls.
② shape & position.
③ oil & sprinkle with paprika.

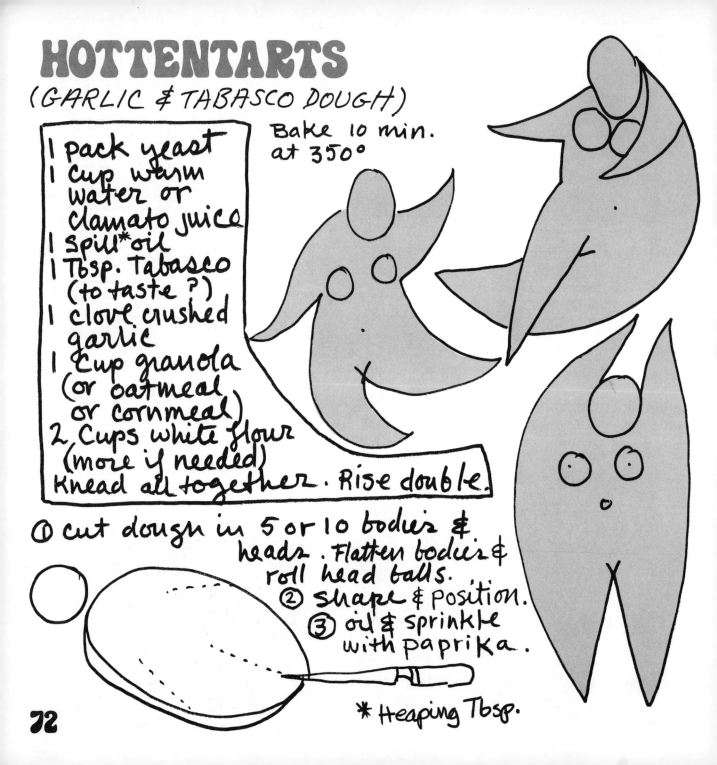

* Heaping Tbsp.

USE SNAKE ROll DOUGH PAGE 32 or

USE preferred dough. Divide into parts.

① shape legs & head, arrange like this...

BEETLE BUNS

② cover legs with flattish pancake back.

③ Add Raisin spots & snip tail.

TURTLE SCONES

① arrange this structure.

② stretch and form muffen back over fingers.

③ cut crisscross on back. snip toes.

73

CROCODILES

The Purity Bakers of Carmel California
are master Crocodile makers...
here is the way they do it—

1. Use any basic bread dough (page 10).
2. After dough has risen 1 hour,
3. Shape 1 large & 2 small Sausages
   as shown, for body & legs.
4. Egg it all over.

75

CROCODILE BUILDING

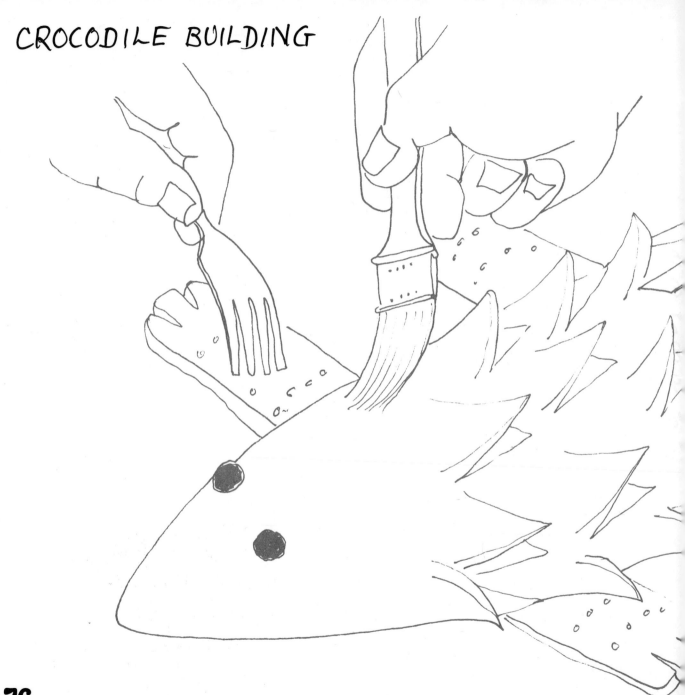

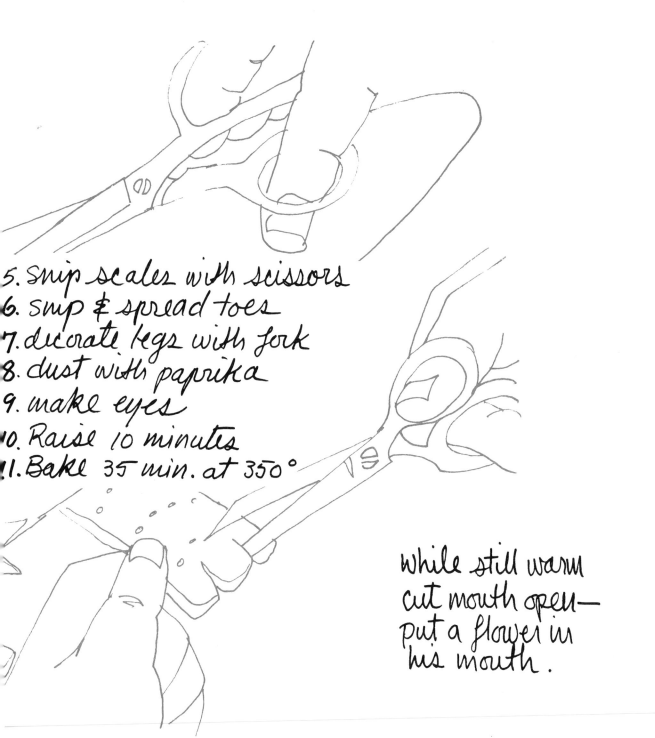

5. snip scales with scissors
6. snip & spread toes
7. decorate legs with fork
8. dust with paprika
9. make eyes
10. Raise 10 minutes
11. Bake 35 min. at 350°

while still warm
cut mouth open—
put a flower in
his mouth.

PEACE PIE

<u>For Pie Crust Lovers</u>
pie dough without
the filling!

2 cups unbleached flour
1 teaspoon salt
2 Tablespoons sugar
1/2 cup oil
1/4 cup water or milk

1. Flip it all together
   lightly with a fork.
2. Roll out dough 1/4"
   thick on baking sheet.
3. Cut dove shape.
4. use scrap dough for tail
   and wing & decorate.

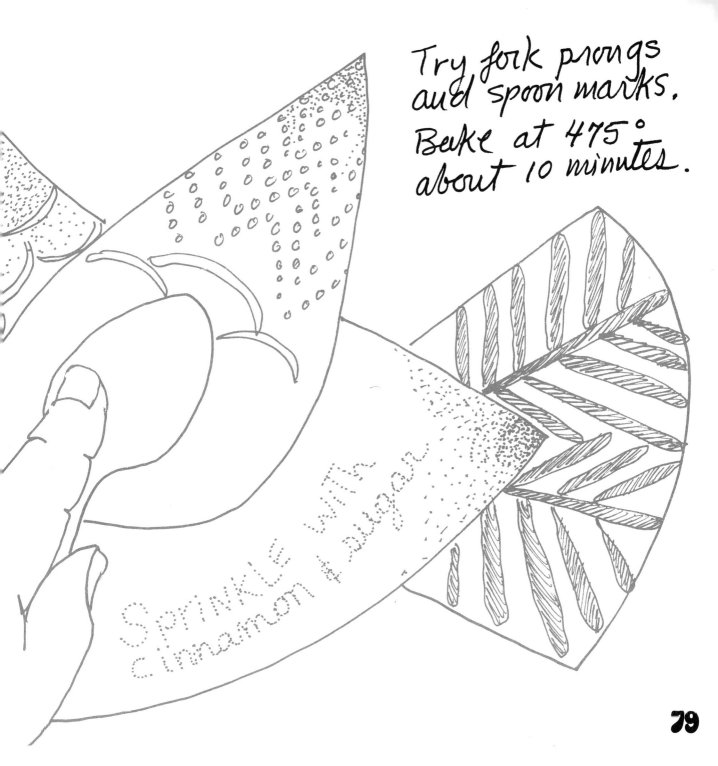

Try fork prongs and spoon marks.
Bake at 475° about 10 minutes.

Sprinkle with cinnamon & sugar

QUICK SODA FLY

<u>No rising - make & bake</u>

½ cup water
1 cup yogurt
   or buttermilk
1 Tablespoon sugar
1 teaspoon salt
1 Egg
1 teaspoon baking powder
1 teaspoon baking soda
2 cups white flour
2 cups whole wheat flour

Knead, shape, bake
at 375°   40 minutes

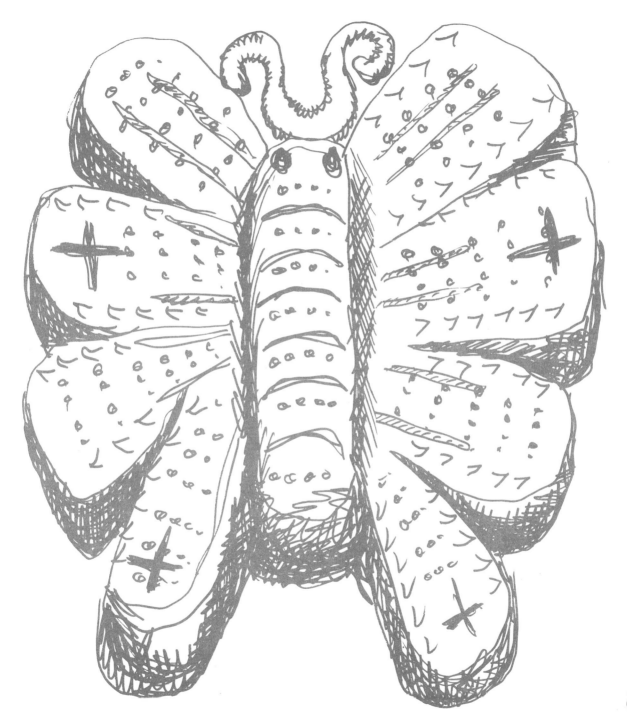

81

FLY BUILDING

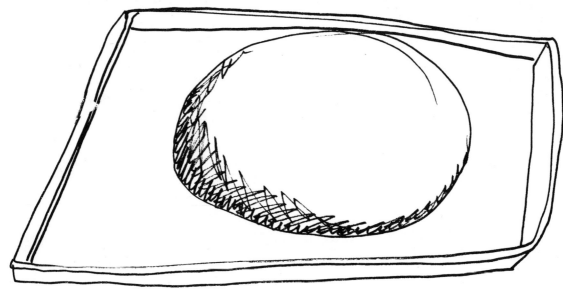

1. Add enough flour to form a dome that holds its shape. Flatten slightly.

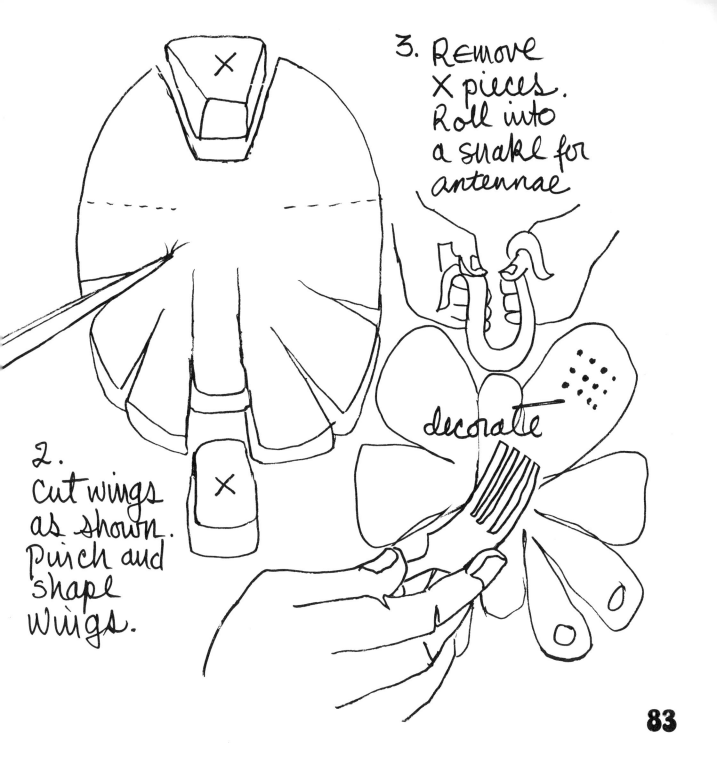

3. Remove X pieces. Roll into a snake for antennae

2. Cut wings as shown. Punch and shape wings.

decorate

GLAD HANDS

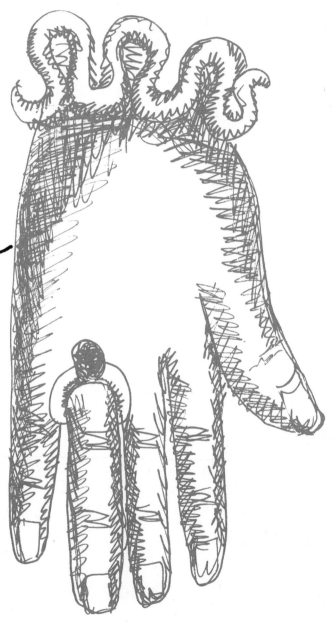

6 to 8 hands

1 cup warm milk
½ cup honey
¼ cup oil or butter
2 eggs
1 teaspoon salt
1 Tablespoon baking powder
½ cup wheat germ
3 or more cups flour,
    unbleached or mixed

Knead in enough
white flour to make
dough non-sticky.
Divide into 8 balls.
Shape & Bake
at 550° 15 to 20 min.

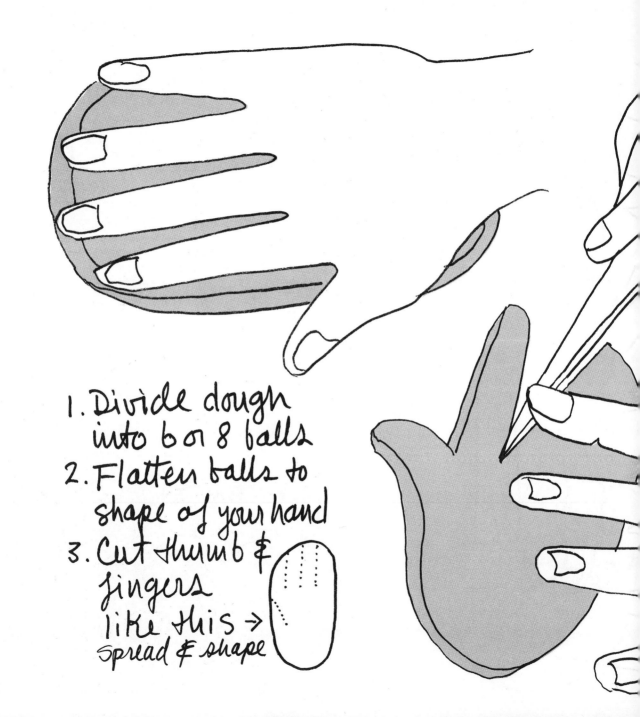

1. Divide dough into 6 or 8 balls
2. Flatten balls to shape of your hand
3. Cut thumb & fingers like this → spread & shape

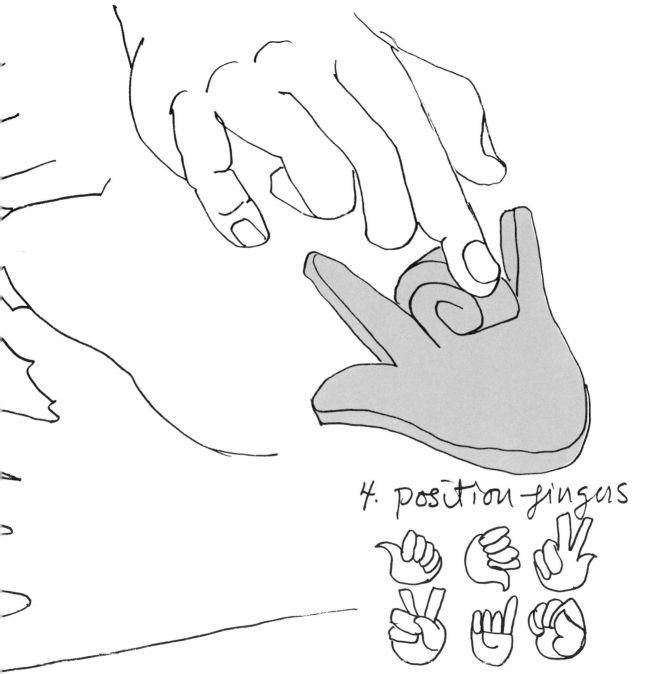

4. position fingers

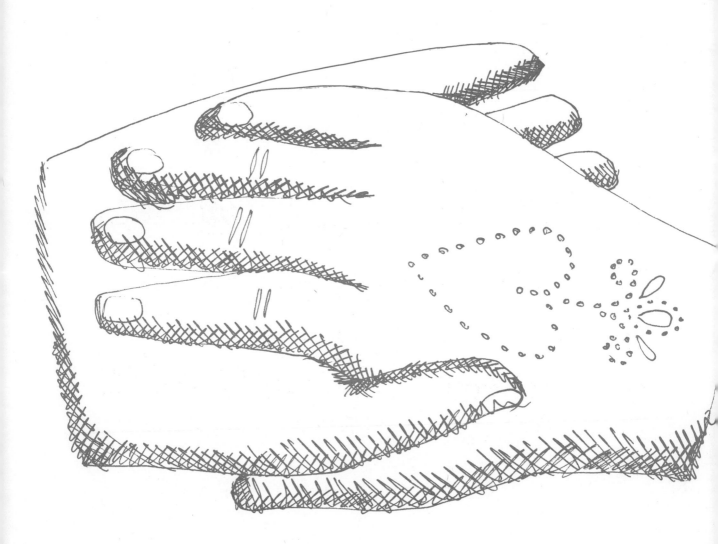

TATTOOED FRIENDSHIP

1. Put Two hands together
2. Tattoo a hopeful heart
3. Bake in good faith
4. And eat with appreciation

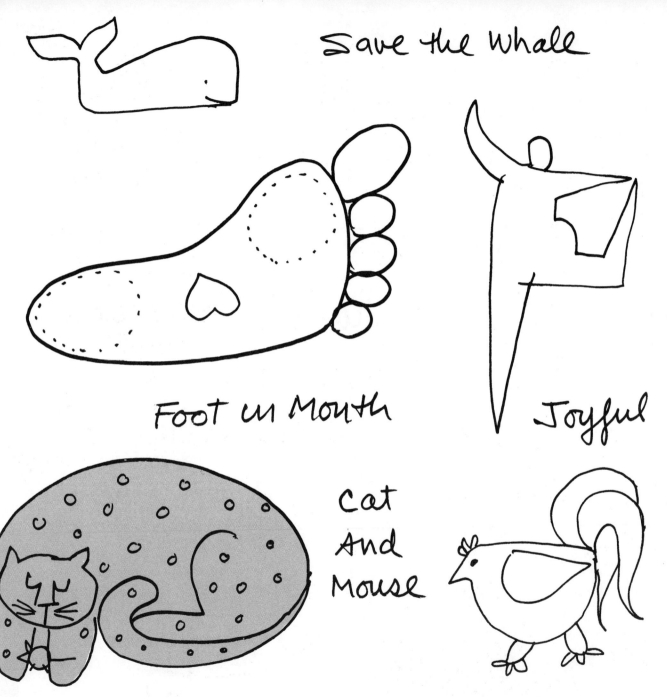

Save the Whale

Foot in Mouth

Joyful

Cat
And
Mouse

MAKE AN OCCASION

Mad
Rabbit

Parvati

Harvest

Peace

NOEL

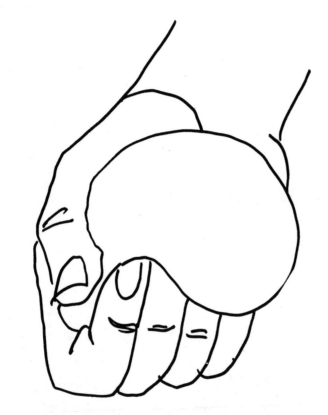

there is no such thing
as mistakes........

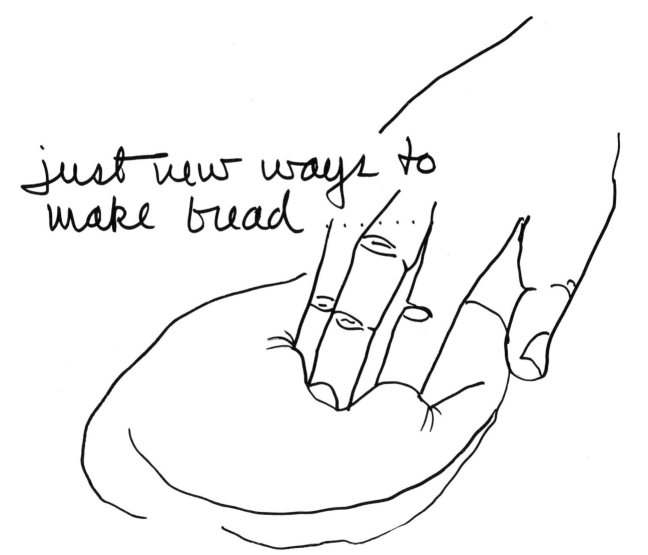

just new ways to
make bread . . . . . .

INDEX

BIOGRAPHICAL NOTES

Ann Wiseman is an artist in many media—painting, kinetic sculpture, hooked tapestries, ceremonial macramé, and now bread sculpture. "I guess it's a question of seeing shapes in any raw material plus a passion for making things. Then there is the fun of sharing it and of helping others find their own creativity."

Her works have been shown in museums and galleries and are in the David Rockefeller and Joseph Hirschhorn collections. She has conducted workshops at numerous schools, colleges and museums. *Bread Sculpture* is her sixth book. Others are: *Making Things: A Hand Book of Creative Discovery* and *Making Things: Book II* (Little Brown); *Rag Tapestries and Wool Mosaics* (Van Nostrand Reinhold); *Rags, Rugs and Wool Pictures* (Scribners); and *Tony's Flower* (Vanguard Press).

Ann Wiseman studied in New York and Paris. She got into bread making when she lived in a French bakery during her student years in Paris. *Life* magazine devoted two pages to one of her bread sculptures in its last issue of December 15, 1972. Presently she lives in Boston and teaches at Leslie College Graduate School in Cambridge, Massachusetts.

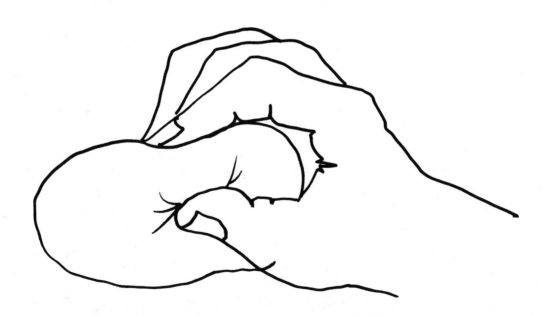